The TEN COMMANDMENTS
The Laws of Love

and The BEATITUDES
The Works of Love

A Coloring Book for Children

Text
Sr. Karen Cavanagh, CSJ

Cover Illustration
Michael Letwenko

Text Illustrations
Edward Letwenko

REGINA PRESS
New York

Who can climb God's mountain? . . . Those who are pure in act and thought, who do not worship idols or make false promises. . . .

God will bless them. God will save them . . . —Ps. 24:3-5

God saved our ancestors and brought Moses and them to Mt. Sinai where a covenant—a promise of love—was made with them.

Like the promise with Abraham and Sarah, God and the people would promise to love one another forever.

Moses became the "great teacher" of God's promise, God's love and God's law—the Ten Commandments.

The commandments were more than laws. They taught how we are to honor and love God and one another.

God's promise and love and law are given to you and me even today.

Each of the commandments shows us how we can show our love for God and for each other.

FIRST COMMANDMENT
DO NOT HAVE FALSE GODS

God is the creator of our world and of each one of us. Nothing is greater than God or God's love. God says, "My love is enough for you."

SECOND COMMANDMENT
Do Not Take God's Name in Vain

Names are special. They say who we are. God's name is very special. We are to respect it and only use it with care and honor.

THIRD COMMANDMENT
REMEMBER GOD'S DAY AND KEEP IT HOLY

On Sunday God wants us to rest and remember who we are. We go to church with our families and friends. We share the day with God and each other.

FOURTH COMMANDMENT
HONOR YOUR FATHER AND YOUR MOTHER

God shares the gift of creation with all people, especially with mothers and fathers. Their love for us is a sign of God's love.

FIFTH COMMANDMENT
DO NOT KILL

Life is a gift from God. When we are kind and caring
and respectful we do not kill life's special times.
Everyone's life is precious.

SIXTH COMMANDMENT
DO NOT COMMIT ADULTERY

Married people are called to be faithful in their promise of love to each other. We are reminded to be true to our friends and our promises.

SEVENTH COMMANDMENT
DO NOT STEAL

Sometimes we would like what belongs to someone else. When we take something from another we hurt the other and do wrong.

EIGHTH COMMANDMENT
Do Not Lie or Hurt Another's Name

Someone always gets hurt when the truth is not told. Sometimes a person is hurt when secrets are told even if they are true.

NINTH COMMANDMENT
DO NOT BE JEALOUS OF ANOTHER'S HUSBAND OR WIFE

Grown up people give the gift of their love as a husband or a wife. This is a very special gift. God does not wish anyone to take this gift from another.

TENTH COMMANDMENT
DO NOT BE JEALOUS OF ANOTHER'S POSSESSIONS

It is all right to want good things for ourselves. It is not good to become unhappy or angry at someone who has what we would like.

Moses was the teacher of the "old law." Jesus ca

God's
OVE

fill God's law and teach us how to live the law.

Jesus is the Word of God. He was the "new teacher" of God and God's law of love.

He loved to have the children gather round Him and listen to the ways of God's love.

Jesus went up the mountainside where he preached to the people. He told of God's kingdom and how it will be different.

He said, "Be happy. . .blessed are you. . . ." You will have the happiness which God can give.

Blessed are the poor in spirit: the reign of God is theirs.

Everything we have is a gift from God. When we remember this we are poor in spirit and rich in thanks.

Blessed are the sorrowing: they shall be comforted.

Jesus promises to be with us in our sadness and sorrow. He is with us in His promise and in the people who love us.

Blessed are the people who are gentle and humble of heart: They shall inherit the land.

When we are patient and keep showing gentle kindness God's happiness will come to us.

Blessed are those who hunger and thirst for holiness: God will satisfy them.

Sometimes we are not praised when we do what is fair and just and caring. Jesus promises to honor us when we are like this.

Blessed are they who show mercy: mercy shall be theirs.

If we help those who are hurting, comfort those who are sad or share what is ours we are showing mercy.

Blessed are the single-hearted: they shall see God.

When God's love is the reason for our love we are able to see God and find God in those we love.

Blessed are the peacemakers: they shall be the daughters and sons of God.

Peacemakers spread God's kingdom not by violence but by love. They speak out against discord and fighting.

Blessed are those who are persecuted for holiness' sake: God's reign is theirs.

Sometimes when we try to be good we are laughed at or rejected. This happened to Jesus, too. God's love is ours.

The commandments and the beatitudes are the Word of God.

We are asked to write them in our hearts and let them become our law of love.

When we write God's law of love in our hearts we also promise to live it in our lives every day.

We trust God's care for us as we live in God's love.

Every day we show our love for God and one another.
We teach God's law of love.

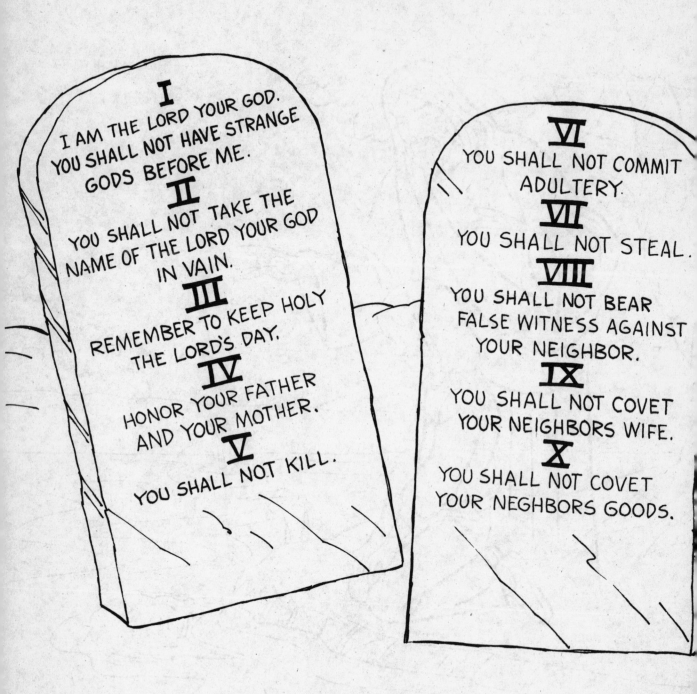

I

I AM THE LORD YOUR GOD.
YOU SHALL NOT HAVE STRANGE
GODS BEFORE ME.

II

YOU SHALL NOT TAKE THE
NAME OF THE LORD YOUR GOD
IN VAIN.

III

REMEMBER TO KEEP HOLY
THE LORD'S DAY.

IV

HONOR YOUR FATHER
AND YOUR MOTHER.

V

YOU SHALL NOT KILL.

VI

YOU SHALL NOT COMMIT
ADULTERY.

VII

YOU SHALL NOT STEAL.

VIII

YOU SHALL NOT BEAR
FALSE WITNESS AGAINST
YOUR NEIGHBOR.

IX

YOU SHALL NOT COVET
YOUR NEIGHBORS WIFE.

X

YOU SHALL NOT COVET
YOUR NEGHBORS GOODS.

We are today's teachers.

When we treat others the way we want to be treated we become beatitude people.

We teach others God's law of love. . . .God will welcome us to heaven.

DRAW YOURSELF LIVING GOD's LAW OF LOVE

WRITE YOUR STORY

_____

_____

_____

_____